Unlocking Organizational Potential

Unlocking Organizational Potential

Dr Livingston

CONTENTS

CONTENTS

Introduction

Welcome to the world of consulting, where knowledge meets strategy, and innovation fuels organizational success. In this book, I invite you to embark on a journey of discovery, as we explore the dynamic field of consulting and delve into the intricacies of driving transformational change.

Allow me to introduce myself. I am Dr Livingston, a seasoned professional with a doctorate in Business Management and over 25 years of experience in the realms of technology and business consulting. Throughout my career, I have had the privilege of working with a diverse range of organizations, guiding them towards achieving their goals and unlocking their true potential.

In this book, I aim to share my insights, knowledge, and practical experiences gained over the years. Together, we will unravel the inner workings of the consulting world, uncovering the strategies and techniques that propel organizations towards sustainable growth and success.

Through these pages, I will take you on a step-by-step journey, starting with the fundamentals of consulting and its crucial role in organizational success. We will explore the different types of consultants, their specialized areas of expertise, and the essential skills and qualities that pave the way for excellence in the field.

We will delve into the process of setting a solid foundation for any consulting project, understanding the organization's goals and conducting a comprehensive analysis to identify areas of improvement and opportunities. With a well-defined consulting plan and approach, we will navigate the complex landscape of change management and implementation, tackling resistance and driving meaningful transformation.

Building strong relationships and effective stakeholder engagement will be a key focus, as we explore the art of collaboration, consensus-building, and conflict resolution. We will uncover the importance of measuring success, establishing key performance indicators, and conducting evaluations to ensure continuous improvement.

Ethical considerations will hold a prominent place in our

discussions, as we explore the responsibilities and challenges faced by consultants in upholding professional conduct, maintaining client confidentiality, and navigating sensitive situations with integrity.

Throughout this book, I will not only share theoretical concepts but also infuse the content with personal anecdotes, real-life case studies, and practical tips garnered from my own experiences in the field. My aim is to provide you with a comprehensive and engaging resource that not only informs but also inspires and motivates you to embark on your own journey as a successful consultant.

I invite you to join me on this enlightening expedition, where we will unravel the secrets of consulting excellence and equip ourselves with the tools and knowledge to make a lasting impact. Let us embark on this transformative voyage together.

Wishing you success and fulfilment in your consulting endeavours.

Introduction to Consulting

Welcome to the captivating world of consulting, where experts unravel mysteries, conquer challenges, and guide organizations toward success. In this chapter, we will embark on an exciting journey that will introduce you to the magic of consulting. Get ready to explore the definition and role of consultants, uncover the vital importance they hold in driving organizational triumphs, and discover the diverse types of consultants who bring their unique expertise to the table. We will also unveil the key skills and qualities that transform good consultants into exceptional ones.

Imagine having a secret weapon—a master problem-solver, strategist, and advisor all in one. That's precisely what a consultant is. These experts possess a rare blend of knowledge, experience, and creativity that empowers them to guide organizations through the toughest challenges. They are like wizards, wielding their expertise to unlock hidden opportunities and banish obstacles that stand in the way of success.

Consultants are more than just professionals—they are superheroes of the business world. They swoop in with their capes of expertise, armed with wisdom and fresh perspectives. Their mission is to offer objective advice, challenge the status quo, and ignite transformative change. They are the navigators who guide organizations through stormy waters, illuminating the path to growth and prosperity.

Organizations rely on consultants for a multitude of reasons. They are the masters of their domains, possessing specialized knowledge and insights that can make all the difference. Here's why consultants are truly indispensable:

Consultants are like virtuosos in their respective fields. They possess deep knowledge and understanding of specific industries and areas, enabling them to provide valuable insights, best practices, and innovative solutions that organizations crave.

Consultants have the superpower of objectivity. They are not bound by internal biases or preconceived notions, allowing them to see things others might miss. Their fresh perspective breathes life into stale ideas, igniting innovation and propelling organizations toward greatness.

Picture consultants as shapeshifters, adapting to organizations' ever-changing needs. They offer flexible solutions, providing access to specialized expertise and resources without the burden of long-term commitments. Whether it's a short-term project or a long-term transformation, consultants are there to save the day.

Consultants are catalysts for change. They challenge the status quo, question established norms, and inject new ideas into organizations. They guide businesses through the intricate process of transformation, helping them embrace innovation and become resilient in an ever-evolving landscape.

The consulting world is a vibrant tapestry, woven together by professionals with diverse skills and expertise. Here are some of the heroes you'll encounter:

Management consultants are the strategic architects, building the foundation for organizational success. They tackle everything from operational efficiency to business transformation, armed with analytical prowess and a vision for greatness.

Strategy consultants are the visionary architects, shaping the destiny of organizations. They help businesses define their strategic direction, identify growth opportunities, and gain a competitive edge in the market.

Human Resources consultants are the guardians of organizational talent. They specialize in areas such as talent acquisition, employee engagement, performance management, and crafting HR strategies that nurture a culture of excellence.

Financial consultants possess the power to unlock the secrets of numbers. They guide organizations in financial management, investment strategies, risk assessment, and navigating the complex world of mergers and acquisitions.

IT consultants are the tech-savvy wizards who harness the power of technology to drive organizations forward. They provide guidance on system implementation, cybersecurity, digital transformation, and crafting IT strategies that propel businesses into the digital age.

The Journey to Becoming a Consulting Hero:
To embark on a successful consulting journey, aspiring heroes must possess certain key skills and qualities. Here are the attributes that separate the good from the extraordinary:

Consultants must wield the power of analysis. They possess sharp minds that can gather, interpret, and synthesize information, drawing meaningful insights from complex data.

Effective consultants are master problem-solvers. They relish in dissecting intricate challenges, identifying root causes, and devising innovative and practical solutions.

Consultants are skilled communicators, capable of translating complex ideas into simple, actionable recommendations. They build strong relationships with clients and stakeholders through active listening, empathy, and collaboration.

The consulting realm is a dynamic one, where adaptability and flexibility are essential. Heroes must thrive in diverse environments, embracing change and seizing new opportunities with agility and grace.

Consultants are guardians of trust and integrity. They hold themselves to the highest ethical standards, ensuring confidentiality, professionalism, and credibility in all interactions.

Welcome to the extraordinary realm of consulting, where superheroes wield their expertise to unravel mysteries, conquer challenges, and guide organizations toward triumph. By understanding the definition, role, and importance of consultants, as well as the diverse types of consulting heroes and the key skills they possess, you've taken your first step into this magical world. In the following chapters, we will delve deeper into the art and science of consulting, exploring methodologies, project management, client engagement, and industry-specific insights. So, embrace your inner hero and get ready for an exhilarating journey that will transform you into an exceptional consultant. The adventure awaits!

3

Case Study: The Strategic Advisor

Case Study Background:

Meet Sarah, a seasoned management consultant with years of experience in the industry. She specializes in providing strategic advice to organizations looking to optimize their performance and achieve sustainable growth. Sarah has worked with various clients across different sectors, helping them navigate complex challenges and capitalize on emerging opportunities. Let's explore how Sarah's expertise and skills have made her an invaluable strategic advisor.

Case Study Scenario:

Sarah was approached by a medium-sized technology company, TechPro Inc., that was facing several challenges. The company was experiencing stagnant growth, increased competition, and a decline in customer satisfaction. The leadership team recognized the need for external guidance and sought Sarah's expertise to help steer the organization in the right direction.

Consultant's Approach and Skills:

Understanding the Client's Needs:
Sarah began by conducting extensive interviews with the leadership team, employees, and key stakeholders to gain a deep understanding of TechPro's goals, challenges, and aspirations. She actively listened and asked probing questions to uncover the underlying issues that were hindering the company's progress.

Analytical Thinking and Problem-Solving:
Drawing upon her analytical skills, Sarah analyzed market trends, competitive dynamics, and customer feedback to identify the root causes of TechPro's challenges. She used various frameworks and tools to dissect complex problems, enabling her to develop data-driven insights and strategic recommendations.

Strategic Vision and Planning:
Based on her analysis, Sarah helped the leadership team redefine TechPro's strategic direction. She facilitated workshops and collaborative sessions to align stakeholders' perspectives and generate innovative ideas. Together, they developed a

clear vision, mission, and strategic objectives that would drive the company's growth and competitive advantage.

Change Management and Execution:
Sarah guided TechPro through the implementation of strategic initiatives. She collaborated closely with the leadership team to develop an action plan that outlined specific goals, milestones, and key performance indicators (KPIs). Additionally, she supported the organization in overcoming resistance to change by fostering open communication, addressing concerns, and involving employees at all levels.

Continuous Learning and Improvement:
Throughout the engagement, Sarah emphasized the importance of continuous learning and improvement. She encouraged TechPro to adopt a culture of innovation, knowledge-sharing, and professional development. Sarah recommended training programs, workshops, and industry events to keep the organization updated on emerging trends and best practices.

Results and Impact:
TechPro experienced a significant turnaround under Sarah's guidance. The company's revenue increased by 25% within the first year, market share expanded, and customer satisfaction improved. The leadership team praised Sarah's ability to bring clarity to complex situations, facilitate collaboration, and drive tangible results. TechPro's success positioned

them as industry leaders and opened doors for future growth opportunities.

Key Takeaways:

Consultants like Sarah play a vital role in helping organizations overcome challenges and achieve their strategic goals.

Effective consultants possess a combination of analytical thinking, problem-solving abilities, strategic vision, and change management skills.

The collaboration between consultants and clients leads to innovative solutions, enhanced performance, and sustainable growth.

Continuous learning and improvement are essential for both consultants and organizations to stay ahead in a dynamic business landscape.

Conclusion:

Sarah's case study highlights the crucial role of consultants in driving organizational success. Through her expertise and strategic guidance, TechPro was able to overcome its challenges and achieve remarkable results. This case study demonstrates the value of consultants who bring specialized knowledge, critical thinking, and a client-centric approach to their engagements. As we delve into subsequent chapters, we will explore more real-world case studies that showcase the diverse applications of consulting in different industries and contexts.

* Note: Name and Company was created for your Imagination

4

Setting the Foundation

Welcome to the adventure of a lifetime—the journey of consulting where we uncover the secrets that make organizations thrive. But before we dive headfirst into the excitement, let's take a moment to lay the groundwork for our expedition. In this chapter, we'll embark on a thrilling quest to set a strong foundation for our consulting project. Get ready to explore the organization's goals and objectives, unravel the mysteries of its inner workings through a comprehensive organizational analysis, discover areas of improvement and untapped opportunities, and craft a roadmap that will guide us to success.

Unveiling the Organization's Dreams:

Every organization has its own dreams—ambitions that

fuel its purpose and drive it forward. As consultants, we become dreamcatchers, seeking to understand and embrace those aspirations. We engage with key stakeholders, listening intently to their stories, visions, and desires. We unravel the organization's goals and objectives like ancient scrolls, uncovering the essence of its mission. It's like embarking on a thrilling treasure hunt, following the clues that will lead us to the heart of the organization's dreams.

Decoding the Organizational Enigma:

Now, it's time to unravel the enigma that is the organization itself. Imagine stepping into a hidden world, where every detail holds significance. We become explorers, armed with a toolkit of analysis techniques, ready to unveil the organization's secrets. We delve into the structure, processes, and culture, peering through the cracks to gain a holistic understanding. It's like being an archaeologist, meticulously unearthing artifacts and piecing them together to reveal a captivating narrative.

We don't stop at surface-level observations—we immerse ourselves in the organization's daily life. Through interviews and surveys, we listen to the voices of its people—the heartbeat of the organization. Their stories become the colors that paint a vivid picture of the challenges and opportunities that lie within. We become detectives, seeking the hidden patterns and connections that hold the key to transformation.

Unleashing the Power of Improvement:

Armed with knowledge and insights, we embark on a mission to ignite positive change. We spot the areas where the organization can shine even brighter, where it can overcome obstacles and seize untapped opportunities. It's like being a visionary, seeing the potential that lies beyond the present reality. We craft strategies to streamline processes, enhance the organizational culture, and elevate the customer experience. We become architects of growth, designing blueprints for success.

Charting the Course to Success:

But a journey without a map is like sailing into the unknown. That's why we develop a consulting plan and approach—a roadmap that guides us towards our destination. We become navigators, plotting the course, and setting the milestones that mark our progress. With clear objectives, well-defined timelines, and a collaborative spirit, we forge a path that ensures our consulting engagement will yield fruitful outcomes.

It's not just about the plan—it's about the adventure. We communicate, collaborate, and adapt along the way. We embrace the unexpected and remain agile in the face of change.

The consulting journey becomes a thrilling expedition, filled with surprises, challenges, and triumphs.

Setting the foundation for a successful consulting project is more than just a theoretical exercise—it's an exhilarating adventure. By understanding the organization's dreams, decoding its enigma, unveiling areas of improvement, and crafting a roadmap for success, we set the stage for transformative change. The next chapter awaits us with the secrets of building strong relationships with clients, where we'll discover how trust, communication, and collaboration lay the groundwork for exceptional consulting journeys. So, strap on your boots and get ready—the consulting adventure has only just begun!

5

Case Study: The Transformational Journey

Case Study Background:

Meet Mark, a seasoned consultant specializing in organizational transformation. Mark was approached by a large manufacturing company, GlobalTech Industries (GTI), that was grappling with declining market share, inefficient processes, and a lack of innovation. The company recognized the need for a comprehensive transformation initiative and sought Mark's expertise to set the foundation for their journey towards sustainable success.

Case Study Scenario:

Upon joining GTI, Mark embarked on an extensive discovery phase to gain a deep understanding of the organization's goals, challenges, and aspirations. Through interviews, data analysis, and observation, he identified key areas that required attention and improvement.

Step 1: Understanding the Organization's Goals and Objectives:

Mark held in-depth discussions with GTI's senior executives, department heads, and frontline employees. He sought to understand the organization's long-term vision, strategic objectives, and desired outcomes. By aligning his efforts with GTI's goals, Mark ensured that his recommendations would contribute directly to the company's success.

Step 2: Conducting a Thorough Organizational Analysis:

To assess GTI's current state, Mark conducted a comprehensive organizational analysis. He reviewed the company's structure, processes, and culture, paying close attention to areas such as communication channels, decision-making, and performance metrics. Mark also conducted surveys and interviews to gather insights from employees at all levels, capturing their perspectives and identifying pain points.

Step 3: Identifying Areas of Improvement and Opportunities:

Based on the findings from the organizational analysis, Mark identified areas of improvement and growth opportunities for GTI. He analyzed the data collected, discerned trends and patterns, and prioritized the challenges that had the greatest impact on GTI's performance. This included streamlining production processes, fostering a culture of innovation, and enhancing customer experience.

Step 4: Developing a Consulting Plan and Approach:
Armed with a comprehensive understanding of GTI's goals and the challenges at hand, Mark developed a consulting plan and approach. The plan outlined the specific objectives, scope of work, timelines, and deliverables of the engagement. It ensured clear communication and alignment between Mark and GTI's leadership, fostering a strong partnership throughout the transformation journey.

Results and Impact:
Under Mark's guidance, GTI experienced a remarkable transformation. The company successfully streamlined its production processes, resulting in improved efficiency and cost savings. The implementation of an innovation framework led to a surge in new product development, boosting GTI's competitiveness in the market. Additionally, customer satisfaction scores increased significantly due to enhanced customer experience initiatives.

The overall impact of the transformation efforts was reflected in GTI's financial performance, with a noticeable increase in revenue and profitability. Employees were more engaged, motivated, and aligned with the company's vision, contributing to a positive shift in the organizational culture.

Key Takeaways:

Understanding the organization's goals and conducting a thorough analysis are essential steps in setting the foundation for a successful consulting project.

Identifying areas of improvement and growth opportunities allows consultants to prioritize and address the most impactful challenges.

Developing a well-defined consulting plan and approach ensures clear communication, alignment, and shared goals between the consultant and the client.

Successful transformation initiatives can result in improved efficiency, innovation, customer satisfaction, and financial performance.

Conclusion:

Mark's case study illustrates the significance of setting a solid foundation in a consulting engagement. Through his comprehensive analysis and strategic approach, GTI underwent a remarkable transformation, positioning the company for long-term success. This case study demonstrates the value of understanding organizational goals, conducting thorough analyses, identifying improvement areas, and developing a well-defined consulting plan. In subsequent chapters, we will explore more case studies that highlight the practical application of these foundational steps in diverse consulting projects.

6

Building Relationships

Welcome to the heart of consulting—the art of building relationships. In this chapter, we will delve into the secrets of creating meaningful connections with clients that go beyond transactional interactions. Building rapport, establishing trust, effective communication, active listening, and managing expectations are the pillars that lay the foundation for successful consulting partnerships. Get ready to unlock the power of relationships that will elevate your consulting journey to new heights.

The Power of Connection:

Consulting is not just about expertise; it's about people. Clients seek more than just technical advice—they yearn for a consultant who understands their unique challenges, listens to their concerns, and collaborates with them as a trusted partner. Building strong relationships is the key to becoming a consultant who is valued, respected, and sought after.

Rapport: The Building Block of Trust:

Rapport is the secret sauce that creates a harmonious connection with clients. It's the art of finding common ground, establishing mutual understanding, and creating an environment where open dialogue can flourish. Through genuine conversations, shared experiences, and a dash of empathy, consultants can lay the foundation for trust and collaboration.

Effective Communication: The Bridge to Success:

Communication is the lifeline of consulting relationships. It's not just about transmitting information—it's about crafting compelling narratives, conveying ideas with impact, and fostering a sense of shared purpose. Effective consultants master the art of tailoring their communication style to connect with clients, ensuring clarity, transparency, and alignment of goals.

Listening with Intent: The Magic of Understanding:

In a world filled with noise, true listening is a rare gift. Active listening is the superpower that enables consultants to truly understand their clients' needs, challenges, and aspirations. By giving undivided attention, reading between the lines, and asking probing questions, consultants can unearth valuable insights that drive meaningful solutions.

Managing Expectations: Navigating the Waters:

Expectations can make or break consulting relationships. Managing them with finesse is a vital skill. Effective consultants set realistic expectations from the start, ensuring clarity on deliverables, timelines, and outcomes. They proactively address concerns, provide regular updates, and navigate through challenges, building trust and confidence along the way

7

Building Relationships

Welcome to the heart of consulting—the art of building relationships. In this chapter, we will delve into the secrets of creating meaningful connections with clients that go beyond transactional interactions. Building rapport, establishing trust, effective communication, active listening, and managing expectations are the pillars that lay the foundation for successful consulting partnerships. Get ready to unlock the power of relationships that will elevate your consulting journey to new heights.

The Power of Connection:

Consulting is not just about expertise; it's about people. Clients seek more than just technical advice—they yearn for a consultant who understands their unique challenges, listens to their concerns, and collaborates with them as a trusted partner. Building strong relationships is the key to becoming a consultant who is valued, respected, and sought after.

Rapport: The Building Block of Trust:

Rapport is the secret sauce that creates a harmonious connection with clients. It's the art of finding common ground, establishing mutual understanding, and creating an environment where open dialogue can flourish. Through genuine conversations, shared experiences, and a dash of empathy, consultants can lay the foundation for trust and collaboration.

Effective Communication: The Bridge to Success:

Communication is the lifeline of consulting relationships. It's not just about transmitting information—it's about crafting compelling narratives, conveying ideas with impact, and fostering a sense of shared purpose. Effective consultants master the art of tailoring their communication style to connect with clients, ensuring clarity, transparency, and alignment of goals.

Listening with Intent: The Magic of Understanding:

In a world filled with noise, true listening is a rare gift. Active listening is the superpower that enables consultants to truly understand their clients' needs, challenges, and aspirations. By giving undivided attention, reading between the lines, and asking probing questions, consultants can unearth valuable insights that drive meaningful solutions.

Managing Expectations: Navigating the Waters:

Expectations can make or break consulting relationships. Managing them with finesse is a vital skill. Effective consultants set realistic expectations from the start, ensuring clarity on deliverables, timelines, and outcomes. They proactively address concerns, provide regular updates, and navigate through challenges, building trust and confidence along the way

8

Case Study: Strengthening Client Partnerships

Case Study Background:

Sarah, an experienced consultant specializing in organizational development, was engaged by a global technology company, Tech Solutions Inc. (TSI). TSI was facing challenges related to employee engagement and organizational culture, and they sought Sarah's expertise to address these issues. Sarah understood that building strong relationships with TSI's leaders and employees was crucial for the success of the project.

Case Study Scenario:

Sarah focused on building relationships with key stakeholders at TSI to foster collaboration, trust, and open communication throughout the engagement. Here's how she navigated the process:

Step 1: Establishing Rapport and Trust with Clients:

Sarah recognized the importance of establishing rapport and trust from the start. She invested time in building personal connections with TSI's leaders, taking a genuine interest in their perspectives, challenges, and aspirations. By demonstrating empathy and understanding, Sarah created a foundation of trust that laid the groundwork for effective collaboration.

Step 2: Effective Communication Strategies:

Sarah understood the significance of clear and concise communication. She ensured that all interactions with TSI's stakeholders were characterized by transparency, active listening, and clarity. Sarah adapted her communication style to suit the preferences of each stakeholder, whether it was face-to-face meetings, email updates, or formal presentations. By tailoring her approach, Sarah maximized engagement and understanding.

Step 3: Active Listening and Understanding Client Needs:

Sarah prioritized active listening as a key communication skill. She engaged in open and honest dialogue with TSI's leaders and employees, actively seeking their input and understanding their needs. By listening attentively, Sarah gained valuable insights into the organization's challenges, enabling her to tailor her recommendations and solutions to address their specific requirements.

Step 4: Managing Client Expectations and Addressing Concerns:

Sarah recognized the importance of managing client expectations throughout the project. She regularly communicated progress updates, milestones, and any potential challenges that arose. Sarah also proactively addressed concerns and feedback from TSI's stakeholders, ensuring their voices were heard and their concerns were addressed promptly. By managing expectations effectively, Sarah maintained a positive and trusting relationship with the client.

Results and Impact:

Through Sarah's efforts in building relationships with TSI's leaders and employees, the project achieved significant outcomes. The engagement led to increased employee engagement and improved organizational culture at TSI. Sarah's collaborative approach and open communication fostered a sense of ownership among employees, leading to higher motivation and productivity levels.

TSI's leaders appreciated Sarah's ability to understand their needs and tailor solutions accordingly. The trust and rapport built with the client allowed for a smooth implementation process and a successful outcome. Overall, Sarah's relationship-building efforts contributed to a positive project experience and long-term partnership with TSI.

Key Takeaways:

- Establishing rapport and trust with clients is essential for successful consulting engagements.
- Effective communication strategies, including active listening and tailored communication, enhance understanding and engagement.
- Understanding client needs through active listening allows consultants to develop customized solutions.
- Managing client expectations and addressing concerns promptly builds trust and maintains a positive relationship.

Conclusion:

Sarah's case study highlights the importance of building strong relationships in the consulting field. By establishing rapport, practicing effective communication, actively listening, and managing client expectations, Sarah created a foundation of trust and collaboration with TSI. This case study demonstrates that building relationships is not just a soft skill but a strategic approach that leads to improved project outcomes and long-term client partnerships. In the following chapters, we will explore additional case studies that showcase the practical application of relationship-building strategies in different consulting contexts.

Data Gathering and Analysis

You're embarking on a consulting journey, armed with the power of data to unlock the secrets that lie within an organization. In this chapter, we dive headfirst into the exhilarating world of data gathering and analysis—a crucial step in uncovering the hidden gems of information that will shape our understanding, problem-solving efforts, and strategic decision-making. Get ready to explore the thrilling process of collecting relevant data, conducting interviews and surveys, analyzing data to unveil patterns and trends, and harnessing the power of tools and techniques for data analysis.

Unveiling the Quest for Data:

Every great consulting adventure starts with collecting the right data—like embarking on a treasure hunt for the key pieces that unlock the organization's mysteries. We scour through mountains of internal documents and records, dusting off financial statements, operational reports, and organizational charts to reveal the organization's history, performance, and current state. We also venture into the external realm, unearthing market research reports, industry publications, and other valuable sources that shed light on market trends, competitors, and best practices. Each piece of data is like a clue, leading us closer to the treasure trove of insights.

Into the Heart of the Organization:

As consultants, we don our investigator hats and dive deep into the organization's inner workings. We step into the shoes of key stakeholders, employees, and customers, seeking their perspectives, experiences, and opinions. Through interviews and surveys, we engage in lively conversations, extracting valuable qualitative data that adds color and depth to our understanding. It's like piecing together a mosaic, as each response reveals a new fragment that contributes to the bigger picture.

Unravelling the Data Tapestry:

Now comes the thrilling part—analyzing the data to unlock its secrets. We become detectives, examining the patterns, trends, and relationships hidden within the numbers and narratives. Armed with visualization tools, statistical wizardry, and data mining techniques, we transform raw data into captivating stories that reveal the organization's challenges and opportunities. It's like decoding a secret message, with each data point providing a clue that brings us closer to cracking the case.

Tools of the Trade:

But fear not, for we have powerful tools at our disposal. Think of them as our trusty sidekicks, assisting us on our consulting journey. With spreadsheet software like Excel or Google Sheets, we organize, clean, and perform basic analysis on the data—tidying it up for the big reveal. We wield data visualization tools like Tableau and Power BI, creating eye-catching charts and graphs that breathe life into the numbers. And with statistical analysis software like SPSS or R, we unleash the full might of statistical prowess, unraveling the intricate relationships hidden within the data tapestry.

The Thrill of Discovery:

As we navigate the twists and turns of data analysis, a sense of anticipation builds. We connect the dots, interpreting the findings, and synthesizing the insights into a comprehensive understanding of the situation. It's like discovering a hidden treasure trove—a eureka moment that shapes the path forward. With each discovery, we unlock the potential for transformation and growth, armed with data-driven recommendations that have the power to propel organizations to new heights.

Next Stop: Problem Identification and Solution Development:

But our journey doesn't end here. In the next chapter, we'll embark on the exhilarating quest of problem identification and solution development. Armed with the insights gained from data analysis, we'll navigate the labyrinth of organizational challenges, designing innovative solutions that address the core issues at hand. Get ready for a rollercoaster ride of creativity, collaboration, and strategic thinking as we chart a course towards organizational success.

So, buckle up and prepare to dive headfirst into the thrilling world of data gathering and analysis—the engine that drives our consulting adventures. With data as our compass, insights as our guide, and tools as our trusted allies, we're ready to unlock the secrets of organizational success, one data point at a time.

10

Case Study: Enhancing Decision-Making through Data

Case Study Background:

Alex, a data analytics consultant, was engaged by a retail company, TrendyStyles, to help improve their inventory management system. The company was facing challenges related to stockouts and excess inventory, leading to lost sales and increased costs. Alex understood that conducting thorough data gathering and analysis was crucial to identify the underlying issues and develop effective solutions.

Case Study Scenario:

Alex employed various data gathering and analysis techniques to gain insights into TrendyStyles' inventory management practices. Here's how Alex approached the process:

Step 1: Collecting Relevant Data and Information:

Alex began by identifying the key data needed to analyze 'TrendyStyles' inventory management system. This involved collecting data on sales, inventory levels, customer demand, supplier lead times, and other relevant factors. Alex collaborated with the company's IT department to ensure the availability and accuracy of the data.

Step 2: Conducting Interviews and Surveys:

To complement the quantitative data, Alex conducted interviews and surveys with TrendyStyles' employees, including store managers, inventory planners, and procurement staff. These qualitative inputs provided valuable context and insights into the challenges and pain points experienced by the company's personnel.

Step 3: Analyzing Data to Identify Patterns and Trends:

Using advanced data analysis tools and techniques, Alex analyzed the collected data to identify patterns and trends. This involved performing statistical analyses, creating visualizations, and conducting exploratory data analysis. Alex sought to uncover correlations between inventory levels, sales performance, and other relevant factors.

Step 4: Utilizing Tools and Techniques for Data Analysis:

Alex utilized various tools and techniques to conduct in-depth data analysis. This included using statistical software packages, data visualization tools, and predictive modeling techniques. By employing these tools, Alex could uncover insights and make data-driven recommendations to improve TrendyStyles' inventory management practices.

Results and Impact:

Through Alex's data gathering and analysis efforts, TrendyStyles gained valuable insights that led to significant improvements in their inventory management system. The analysis revealed that certain product categories experienced consistently high demand, while others were prone to seasonality or fluctuations. This insight allowed the company to optimize their inventory levels and allocate resources more effectively.

Additionally, by analyzing supplier lead times and order fulfillment processes, Alex identified opportunities to streamline the supply chain and reduce stockouts. These improvements resulted in enhanced customer satisfaction, increased sales, and reduced costs associated with excess inventory.

Key Takeaways:

Collecting relevant data and information is essential for understanding the current state of a problem or challenge.

Conducting interviews and surveys provides valuable qualitative insights that complement quantitative data analysis. Analyzing data helps identify patterns, correlations, and trends that inform decision-making. Utilizing tools and techniques for data analysis enables more accurate and insightful findings.

Conclusion:

Alex's case study illustrates the importance of data

gathering and analysis in the consulting process. By collecting relevant data, conducting interviews and surveys, analyzing the data, and utilizing tools and techniques, Alex was able to provide TrendyStyles with actionable insights to improve their inventory management system. This case study demonstrates how data-driven decision-making can lead to significant improvements in business processes and outcomes. In the following chapters, we will explore additional case studies that showcase the practical application of data gathering and analysis techniques in diverse consulting scenarios.

11

Unveiling Opportunities

Welcome to the exhilarating world of problem-solving and solution development. In this chapter, we will embark on a journey to identify key issues and challenges within organizations and transform them into opportunities for growth and success. We will dive into the art of problem identification, prioritization, brainstorming innovative solutions, and crafting a comprehensive action plan. Get ready to unleash your creativity and strategic thinking as we unravel the path to overcoming obstacles and achieving remarkable results.

The Art of Problem Identification:

Problems are the gateways to progress. Consultants possess the unique ability to identify and unravel the underlying issues that hinder organizational performance. Through a blend of analytical thinking, deep insights, and a dash of intuition, they shine a light on the areas that require attention. The art lies in asking the right questions, challenging assumptions, and peering beneath the surface to discover the true root causes.

Prioritization: Focusing on Impact and Feasibility:

Not all problems are created equal. Effective consultants understand the importance of prioritization to ensure efficient resource allocation and maximum impact. By assessing the potential impact of each problem and evaluating the feasibility of solving them, consultants can strategically prioritize their efforts, tackling the most pressing issues first and laying the groundwork for transformative change.

Unleashing the Power of Innovation:

In the realm of problem-solving, innovation reigns supreme. Consultants are catalysts for creativity, pushing boundaries, and thinking outside the box. Through collaborative brainstorming sessions, they gather diverse perspectives, unlock fresh ideas, and generate innovative solutions. It is in this fertile ground that breakthrough strategies and game-changing initiatives take shape.

Crafting a Comprehensive Action Plan:

Ideas without execution are merely dreams. A comprehensive action plan is the blueprint that guides organizations from vision to reality. Consultants meticulously craft a roadmap that outlines the steps, resources, timelines, and milestones required to implement their recommendations. This plan ensures clarity, accountability, and alignment with the organization's objectives, setting the stage for tangible results.

The Power of Collaboration:

Solving complex problems requires collective wisdom and collaboration. Effective consultants understand the value of engaging stakeholders, leveraging their expertise, and fostering a culture of shared ownership. By involving key players throughout the problem identification and solution development process, consultants tap into the collective intelligence of the organization, fostering buy-in, and increasing the likelihood of successful implementation.

Problem identification and solution development are at the heart of consulting's transformative power. By mastering the art of problem identification, prioritization, brainstorming innovative solutions, and crafting a comprehensive action plan, consultants become architects of change. They navigate the complexities of organizational challenges, unveiling opportunities for growth and success. As we move forward in our consulting journey, we will explore the intricacies of implementation, change management, and the art of delivering lasting impact. Get ready to unleash your problem-solving prowess and pave the way for a brighter future!

12

Case Study: Transforming Customer Service for Better Satisfaction

Case Study Background:

Sarah, a management consultant specializing in customer experience, was hired by a telecommunications company, ConnectTel, to address their declining customer satisfaction ratings. The company had received numerous complaints about long wait times, ineffective issue resolution, and poor overall service. Sarah understood the importance of accurately identifying the key issues and developing innovative solutions to enhance customer service.

Case Study Scenario:

Sarah followed a systematic approach to problem

identification and solution development. Here's how she tackled the process:

Step 1: Identifying Key Issues and Challenges:
Sarah began by conducting interviews with ConnectTel's customer service representatives, analyzing customer feedback data, and observing customer interactions. Through this comprehensive assessment, Sarah identified several key issues, including understaffed call centers, outdated customer service technology, and inadequate training programs.

Step 2: Prioritizing Problems Based on Impact and Feasibility:
To prioritize the identified issues, Sarah assessed their impact on customer satisfaction and the feasibility of addressing them. She analyzed customer feedback ratings, call center metrics, and employee feedback to determine the severity of each problem. This allowed her to focus on the issues that would have the most significant impact on improving customer service.

Step 3: Brainstorming and Generating Innovative Solutions:
Sarah facilitated brainstorming sessions with cross-functional teams, including customer service representatives, IT specialists, and operations managers. Together, they generated innovative ideas to address the identified issues. Sarah encouraged an open and collaborative environment, where

everyone's input was valued, leading to a diverse range of solutions.

Step 4: Developing a Comprehensive Action Plan:

Based on the brainstorming sessions, Sarah developed a comprehensive action plan. This plan included specific initiatives such as implementing a customer relationship management (CRM) system to improve call center efficiency, introducing personalized training programs to enhance employee skills, and redesigning the customer feedback process for quicker resolution of issues.

Results and Impact:

By diligently following the problem identification and solution development process, Sarah helped ConnectTel achieve significant improvements in customer service. The implementation of a CRM system reduced call center wait times by 30%, resulting in a higher rate of first-call resolutions. The personalized training programs improved the skills and confidence of customer service representatives, leading to more effective issue resolution and higher customer satisfaction ratings.

Additionally, the redesigned customer feedback process allowed ConnectTel to promptly address customer concerns and proactively identify areas for improvement. This approach led to an increase in customer loyalty and positive word-of-mouth, ultimately contributing to business growth and success.

Key Takeaways:

- Identifying key issues and challenges requires a thorough assessment of customer feedback, employee insights, and data analysis.
- Prioritizing problems based on impact and feasibility helps focus resources and efforts on areas that will have the most significant impact.
- Brainstorming and generating innovative solutions involve involving cross-functional teams to encourage diverse perspectives and ideas.
- Developing a comprehensive action plan ensures that the identified solutions are implemented effectively and systematically.

Conclusion:

Sarah's case study exemplifies the importance of problem identification and solution development in the consulting process. By accurately identifying the key issues, prioritizing them, brainstorming innovative solutions, and developing a comprehensive action plan, Sarah helped ConnectTel transform their customer service and improve overall customer satisfaction. This case study underscores the value of addressing customer-centric challenges and developing tailored solutions to enhance organizational performance. In the following chapters, we will explore additional case studies that demonstrate the practical application of problem identification and solution development techniques in various consulting contexts.

13

Embracing the Winds of Change

Change is the only constant in today's dynamic business landscape. In this chapter, we will embark on a transformative journey into change management and implementation, exploring the intricacies of guiding organizations through periods of transition and driving successful change initiatives. We will delve into the significance of change management, overcoming resistance to change, creating a detailed implementation strategy, and the art of monitoring progress and making necessary adjustments. Prepare to embrace the winds of change and navigate the path to organizational resilience and growth.

The Significance of Change Management:

Change without effective management is like sailing into uncharted waters without a compass. Change management is the compass that ensures organizations stay on course during periods of transition. It encompasses a systematic approach to preparing, equipping, and supporting individuals and teams to adopt new behaviors, processes, and mindsets. By embracing change management principles, consultants can mitigate risks, minimize disruption, and maximize the chances of successful change implementation.

Overcoming Resistance to Change:

Change is often met with resistance, as human nature tends to cling to familiarity and routine. Consultants play a pivotal role in navigating this resistance and fostering a culture of openness and adaptability. They employ various strategies such as effective communication, stakeholder engagement, and addressing fears and concerns head-on. By building trust, creating a compelling case for change, and involving employees in the change process, consultants can turn resistance into resilience.

Creating a Detailed Implementation Strategy:

Successful change implementation requires a well-crafted and comprehensive strategy. Consultants meticulously plan each phase of the implementation journey, taking into account the unique needs and dynamics of the organization. This strategy outlines the key activities, resources, timelines, and milestones required to bring about the desired change. It sets the stage for a smooth transition, ensuring that all stakeholders are aligned and empowered to embrace the new direction.

Monitoring Progress and Making Necessary Adjustments:

Change is a dynamic process that requires continuous monitoring and adjustment. Consultants keep a vigilant eye on the progress of change initiatives, tracking key metrics, and evaluating the effectiveness of implemented strategies. By identifying early warning signs and addressing challenges proactively, consultants can make necessary adjustments to keep the change effort on track. This iterative approach allows for agility and course correction, maximizing the chances of achieving desired outcomes.

The Power of Leadership:

Change management relies heavily on strong leadership at

all levels of the organization. Consultants work closely with leaders to ensure they are equipped with the necessary skills and mindset to drive change effectively. Leaders set the tone, communicate the vision, and inspire their teams to embrace the change. By cultivating a supportive and empowering leadership culture, consultants lay the foundation for successful change management and implementation.

Change management and implementation are the bridges that connect vision and reality. By understanding the significance of change management, overcoming resistance, creating a detailed implementation strategy, and continuously monitoring progress, consultants become agents of transformation. They guide organizations through the winds of change, fostering resilience, and driving success. As we move forward in our consulting journey, we will explore the power of effective communication, the art of building high-performing teams, and the nuances of sustaining change for long-term impact. Get ready to embrace change and unlock the potent

14

Case Study: Implementing a New Performance Management System

Case Study Background:

Emily, a change management consultant, was hired by a large manufacturing company, GlobalTech, to implement a new performance management system across the organization. The company recognized the need for a more streamlined and effective process to evaluate employee performance, set goals, and provide feedback. Emily understood the importance of change management in ensuring successful implementation and addressing resistance to change.

Case Study Scenario:

Emily followed a structured approach to change management and implementation. Let's explore her process in detail:

Step 1: Understanding the Importance of Change Management:

Emily began by emphasizing the significance of change management to the leadership team at GlobalTech. She explained that a successful implementation requires not only a well-designed performance management system but also a strategic approach to address the human side of change. Emily stressed that effective change management would help minimize resistance and ensure employee buy-in.

Step 2: Overcoming Resistance to Change:

Emily conducted stakeholder analysis to identify potential sources of resistance and understand the concerns of different employee groups. She held workshops and communication sessions to address their questions and fears, emphasizing the benefits of the new performance management system. Emily actively engaged employees throughout the process, seeking their input and involving them in decision-making to build a sense of ownership.

Step 3: Creating a Detailed Implementation Strategy:

Emily developed a comprehensive implementation strategy that outlined the key steps, timelines, and responsibilities. She collaborated with the HR department to design training programs for managers and employees to familiarize them with the new system. The strategy also included clear communication plans, highlighting the purpose, benefits, and expectations of the new performance management system.

Step 4: Monitoring Progress and Making Necessary Adjustments:

During the implementation phase, Emily closely monitored the progress of the new performance management system. She conducted regular feedback sessions and surveys to gather employee input and address any concerns or challenges. Based on this feedback, Emily made necessary adjustments to the implementation strategy, such as providing additional training resources or clarifying certain aspects of the system.

Results and Impact:

Thanks to Emily's diligent change management and implementation efforts, GlobalTech successfully transitioned to the new performance management system. Employee engagement and participation increased significantly, and managers felt more equipped to provide constructive feedback and support employee development. The new system also allowed for more objective and fair performance evaluations, leading to improved individual and organizational performance.

By addressing resistance to change, providing clear communication, and actively involving employees, Emily ensured that the implementation process was smooth and successful. The change management approach helped create a positive and supportive environment, encouraging employees to embrace the new performance management system.

Key Takeaways:

- Understanding the importance of change management is crucial to navigate the human side of change and ensure successful implementation.
- Overcoming resistance to change requires stakeholder analysis, effective communication, and involving employees in the decision-making process.
- Creating a detailed implementation strategy helps guide the process, set expectations, and allocate resources effectively.
- Monitoring progress and making necessary adjustments based on feedback and insights helps address challenges and improve implementation outcomes.

Conclusion:

Emily's case study highlights the significance of change management in implementing new initiatives within organizations. By understanding the importance of change management, overcoming resistance to change, creating a detailed implementation strategy, and monitoring progress, Emily ensured the successful adoption of a new performance management system at GlobalTech. This case study emphasizes the importance of actively managing the people side of change to achieve desired outcomes. In the following chapters, we will explore additional case studies that illustrate the practical application of change management and implementation strategies in diverse consulting contexts.

15

Unleashing the Power of Collaboration

In today's interconnected and interdependent business landscape, stakeholder engagement and collaboration have become critical drivers of organizational success. In this chapter, we will embark on a journey of unlocking the power of collaboration, exploring the art of engaging stakeholders at different levels, building effective teams and partnerships, facilitating collaboration and consensus-building, and mastering the skill of managing conflicts and resolving disputes. Get ready to break down silos, foster synergy, and unleash the collective intelligence of your organization.

Engaging Stakeholders at Different Levels:

Stakeholders are the lifeblood of any organization, and

effective stakeholder engagement is the key to harnessing their potential. Consultants employ various strategies to engage stakeholders at different levels, from executives to frontline employees, customers, suppliers, and community members. They create platforms for open dialogue, gather diverse perspectives, and ensure that stakeholders' voices are heard and valued. By actively involving stakeholders in decision-making processes, consultants tap into the collective wisdom of the organization, leading to more informed and sustainable outcomes.

Building Effective Teams and Partnerships:

Behind every successful project or initiative lies a high-performing team. Consultants understand the importance of assembling teams with complementary skills, diverse perspectives, and a shared sense of purpose. They foster an environment of trust, collaboration, and mutual respect, where individuals can contribute their best and leverage each other's strengths. Additionally, consultants also facilitate partnerships with external stakeholders, such as vendors, industry experts, and community organizations, to broaden the scope of knowledge and resources available.

Facilitating Collaboration and Consensus-Building:

Collaboration is the fuel that powers innovation and breakthrough thinking. Consultants facilitate collaboration by creating structured frameworks and processes that enable stakeholders to work together towards common goals. They employ techniques such as brainstorming sessions, workshops, and cross-functional working groups to foster creativity, encourage open dialogue, and generate new ideas. Consultants also guide stakeholders in the journey of consensus-building, helping them find common ground and make informed decisions that benefit the organization as a whole.

Managing Conflicts and Resolving Disputes:

Conflicts and disputes are inevitable in any collaborative endeavor. However, effective consultants are skilled in managing conflicts and transforming them into opportunities for growth and understanding. They employ conflict resolution techniques, such as active listening, mediation, and negotiation, to address disagreements and find win-win solutions. By creating a safe and supportive environment for open dialogue, consultants encourage stakeholders to express their concerns, share perspectives, and work towards mutually beneficial resolutions.

The Power of Diversity and Inclusion:

Diversity and inclusion are catalysts for innovation and creativity. Consultants recognize the value of diverse perspectives and ensure that all stakeholders have a seat at the table. They promote inclusivity by fostering a culture that celebrates differences and embraces the richness of varied backgrounds, experiences, and viewpoints. By harnessing the power of diversity, consultants unlock the full potential of collaboration, leading to more robust and sustainable solutions.

Stakeholder engagement and collaboration are the cornerstones of a thriving and resilient organization. By engaging stakeholders at different levels, building effective teams and partnerships, facilitating collaboration and consensus-building, and managing conflicts with grace and integrity, consultants become catalysts of positive change. They break down barriers, foster synergy, and create an environment where diverse voices can flourish. As we continue on our consulting journey, we will explore the art of effective communication, the science of influence and persuasion, and the strategies for sustaining stakeholder engagement over the long term. Get ready to unleash the power of collaboration and propel your organization towards new heights of success!

16

Case Study: Implementing a Sustainability Initiative

Case Study Background:

Sarah, a consultant specializing in sustainability, was engaged by a global retail company, EcoGoods, to implement a sustainability initiative across its supply chain. The initiative aimed to reduce environmental impact, promote ethical sourcing, and enhance social responsibility. Sarah understood the importance of stakeholder engagement and collaboration to ensure the successful implementation of the sustainability initiative.

Case Study Scenario:

Sarah employed various strategies to engage stakeholders and foster collaboration throughout the implementation process. Let's explore her approach in detail:

Step 1: Engaging Stakeholders at Different Levels:

Sarah identified the key stakeholders involved in the sustainability initiative, including senior executives, department managers, suppliers, and employees. She conducted stakeholder analysis to understand their interests, concerns, and level of influence. Sarah then developed tailored communication plans to engage each stakeholder group effectively. She scheduled meetings, workshops, and presentations to ensure their active participation and input.

Step 2: Building Effective Teams and Partnerships:

Sarah recognized the importance of building effective teams and partnerships to drive the sustainability initiative forward. She facilitated the formation of a cross-functional project team comprising representatives from different departments, such as procurement, operations, and marketing. Sarah encouraged collaboration and knowledge sharing among team members, leveraging their diverse expertise to develop innovative and sustainable solutions.

Step 3: Facilitating Collaboration and Consensus-Building:

To facilitate collaboration, Sarah organized regular meetings and workshops where stakeholders could share ideas, perspectives, and best practices. She employed interactive techniques such as brainstorming sessions, group discussions, and team-building exercises to foster a sense of camaraderie and trust among participants. Sarah ensured that all stakeholders had an opportunity to contribute to the decision-making process and reach consensus on key sustainability initiatives.

Step 4: Managing Conflicts and Resolving Disputes:

Throughout the implementation, Sarah encountered conflicts and disputes among stakeholders with differing priorities and perspectives. She adopted a proactive approach to address these conflicts, actively listening to all parties involved and facilitating open dialogue. Sarah sought win-win solutions that aligned with the overall goals of the sustainability initiative. She encouraged stakeholders to find common ground and emphasized the benefits of collaboration and compromise.

Results and Impact:

Sarah's stakeholder engagement and collaboration efforts had a significant impact on the successful implementation of the sustainability initiative at EcoGoods. The active involvement of stakeholders at different levels resulted in a shared vision and commitment to sustainability goals. Cross-functional collaboration led to the identification and implementation of innovative strategies, such as eco-friendly packaging solutions and responsible sourcing practices.

By fostering collaboration and consensus-building, Sarah ensured that the sustainability initiative gained traction and support from stakeholders across the organization. Conflicts and disputes were effectively managed through open communication and a focus on finding mutually beneficial solutions. As a result, EcoGoods achieved measurable improvements in its environmental and social performance, enhancing its brand reputation and customer loyalty.

Key Takeaways:

- Engaging stakeholders at different levels is crucial for the successful implementation of initiatives.
- Building effective teams and partnerships enables collaboration and leverage diverse expertise.
- Facilitating collaboration and consensus-building fosters a shared vision and commitment among stakeholders.
- Managing conflicts and disputes requires active listening, open dialogue, and seeking win-win solutions.

Conclusion:

Sarah's case study highlights the importance of stakeholder engagement and collaboration in implementing sustainability initiatives. By engaging stakeholders at different levels, building effective teams and partnerships, facilitating collaboration, and managing conflicts, Sarah ensured the successful implementation of the sustainability initiative at EcoGoods. This case study emphasizes the value of involving stakeholders in decision-making and fostering a collaborative environment to drive positive change. In the following chapters, we will explore additional case studies that illustrate effective stakeholder engagement and collaboration in various consulting contexts.

17

Unleashing the Power of Results

In the dynamic world of consulting, measuring success and evaluating outcomes is essential for driving continuous improvement and delivering tangible results. In this chapter, we will embark on a journey of harnessing the power of results, exploring the art of establishing key performance indicators (KPIs), tracking progress and measuring outcomes, conducting post-implementation evaluations, and making recommendations for further improvements. Get ready to dive into the realm of meaningful measurement and unleash the true potential of your consulting projects.

Establishing Key Performance Indicators (KPIs):

Like a compass guiding us on our consulting journey,

key performance indicators (KPIs) are essential for measuring progress and aligning efforts with desired outcomes. Consultants work closely with stakeholders to define clear and measurable KPIs that reflect the organization's strategic objectives. By establishing KPIs that are specific, achievable, and relevant, consultants create a roadmap for success and provide a framework for evaluating the impact of their interventions.

Tracking Progress and Measuring Outcomes:

Tracking progress and measuring outcomes is like a heartbeat that keeps the consulting project alive and pulsating with energy. Consultants employ various monitoring and evaluation techniques to gauge the effectiveness of their interventions. They collect data, both quantitative and qualitative, through surveys, interviews, and performance metrics. By analyzing this data, consultants can identify trends, assess the achievement of KPIs, and determine the overall impact of their consulting efforts.

Conducting Post-Implementation Evaluations:

Just as a symphony's finale determines its greatness, post-implementation evaluations are the grand finale of a consulting project. Consultants conduct thorough evaluations to assess the sustainability and long-term impact of their interventions. They examine factors such as stakeholder satisfaction, organizational performance, and the extent to which desired outcomes have been achieved. By conducting comprehensive evaluations, consultants gather insights that inform future decision-making, validate the effectiveness of their recommendations, and lay the groundwork for continuous improvement.

Making Recommendations for Further Improvements:

Consulting projects are not static entities but living organisms that evolve and adapt over time. Based on the findings of evaluations and ongoing monitoring, consultants make recommendations for further improvements and refinements. These recommendations may include adjustments to strategies, process optimizations, talent development initiatives, or changes to organizational structures. By offering insights and recommendations for continuous improvement, consultants ensure that their interventions have a lasting impact and that organizations continue to thrive long after the project's completion.

From Data to Insights:

While data and metrics are the building blocks, the true power lies in transforming them into meaningful insights. Effective consultants go beyond surface-level analysis and delve deep into the data to uncover hidden patterns, trends, and opportunities. They provide clients with actionable insights and strategic recommendations that go beyond numbers and charts. By translating data into meaningful stories, consultants empower organizations to make informed decisions and drive impactful change.

Measuring success and evaluating outcomes are essential components of any consulting project. By establishing clear KPIs, tracking progress, conducting post-implementation evaluations, and providing recommendations for further improvements, consultants unleash the power of results. They transform raw data into meaningful insights and help organizations navigate the path of continuous improvement. As we conclude our journey through the world of consulting, we will explore the art of knowledge transfer, the importance of sustainability, and the strategies for building long-term partnerships with clients. Get ready to unleash the power of results and leave a lasting impact on the organizations you serve!

18

Case Study: Enhancing Customer Satisfaction in a Service Industry

Case Study Background:

John, a consultant specializing in customer experience, was hired by a leading service company, Stellar Services, to enhance customer satisfaction and loyalty. John understood the importance of measuring success and conducting evaluations to ensure the effectiveness of customer satisfaction initiatives.

Case Study Scenario:

John implemented a comprehensive approach to measure success and evaluate the impact of customer satisfaction initiatives. Let's explore his approach in detail:

Step 1: Establishing Key Performance Indicators (KPIs):

John collaborated with Stellar Services to define and establish relevant KPIs aligned with their customer satisfaction goals. These KPIs included metrics such as Net Promoter Score (NPS), customer retention rate, service response time, and customer feedback ratings. By selecting appropriate KPIs, John ensured that the measurement process focused on the essential aspects of customer satisfaction.

Step 2: Tracking Progress and Measuring Outcomes:

To track progress and measure outcomes, John implemented a systematic data collection process. He designed customer surveys, feedback mechanisms, and implemented data analytics tools to gather quantitative and qualitative data. By analyzing this data regularly, John could monitor customer satisfaction levels, identify trends, and measure the impact of customer satisfaction initiatives.

Step 3: Conducting Post-Implementation Evaluations:

Once customer satisfaction initiatives were implemented, John conducted post-implementation evaluations to assess their effectiveness. He compared the actual outcomes against the established KPIs and evaluated the extent to which the initiatives met customer expectations. John conducted surveys, focus groups, and interviews with customers and employees to gather insights and feedback on their experiences.

Step 4: Making Recommendations for Further Improvements:

Based on the evaluation findings, John identified areas for improvement and made recommendations to enhance customer satisfaction further. He presented actionable insights to Stellar Services, highlighting potential changes in processes, training programs, and service delivery. John also suggested strategies for addressing specific pain points and customer concerns, aiming to create a seamless and delightful customer experience.

Results and Impact:

John's approach to measuring success and evaluation resulted in significant improvements in customer satisfaction for Stellar Services. By establishing KPIs and tracking progress, John provided the company with actionable data-driven insights. Through post-implementation evaluations, he identified specific areas where the customer satisfaction initiatives had the most impact and areas that required further attention.

Based on John's recommendations, Stellar Services implemented targeted improvements, such as streamlining service processes, enhancing employee training, and introducing personalized customer engagement strategies. As a result, customer satisfaction scores and NPS increased, leading to higher customer retention rates and positive word-of-mouth recommendations. Stellar Services gained a competitive edge by providing exceptional customer experiences.

Key Takeaways:

- Establishing relevant KPIs is essential to measure success and evaluate customer satisfaction initiatives.
- Tracking progress and measuring outcomes through data collection and analysis provides valuable insights.
- Conducting post-implementation evaluations helps assess the effectiveness of initiatives and identify areas for improvement.
- Making recommendations for further improvements based on evaluation findings ensures continuous enhancement of customer satisfaction.

Conclusion:

John's case study demonstrates the importance of measuring success and conducting evaluations to enhance customer satisfaction in a service industry. By establishing KPIs, tracking progress, conducting evaluations, and making recommendations for further improvements, John helped Stellar Services achieve significant enhancements in customer satisfaction and loyalty. This case study underscores the value of data-driven decision-making and continuous improvement in delivering exceptional customer experiences. In the following chapters, we will explore additional case studies that highlight effective measurement and evaluation strategies in diverse consulting contexts.

19

The Journey of Growth and Transformation

Unlocking the Power of Continuous Learning

In the ever-evolving landscape of consulting, embracing continuous learning and professional development is not just a choice; it is a way of life. In this chapter, we embark on a transformative journey, exploring the importance of ongoing learning and skill development. We will delve into the art of staying updated with industry trends and best practices, seeking feedback, incorporating lessons learned, and building a vibrant professional network that fuels growth and success. Get ready to unlock the power of continuous learning and embark on a path of endless possibilities.

The Importance of Ongoing Learning and Skill Development:

In the fast-paced world we live in, the only constant is change. To thrive in the consulting realm, consultants must recognize the significance of ongoing learning and skill development. By continuously expanding their knowledge and honing their skills, consultants stay ahead of the curve and remain relevant in an ever-changing landscape. Ongoing learning enhances their expertise, fuels innovation, and enables them to provide cutting-edge solutions to their clients. It is the catalyst for personal and professional growth, empowering consultants to tackle new challenges and seize emerging opportunities.

Staying Updated with Industry Trends and Best Practices:

To navigate the ever-shifting currents of the consulting industry, staying updated with industry trends and best practices is paramount. Consultants immerse themselves in industry publications, attend conferences, and participate in webinars and workshops. They seek out thought leaders, engage in discussions, and explore emerging technologies and methodologies. By staying informed, consultants remain at the forefront of industry advancements, enabling them to offer the latest insights and deliver exceptional value to their clients.

Seeking Feedback and Incorporating Lessons Learned:

In the realm of continuous learning, feedback is the fuel that propels growth and improvement. Effective consultants actively seek feedback from clients, colleagues, and stakeholders. They embrace constructive criticism and view it as an opportunity for growth. Consultants also engage in self-reflection, analyzing their own performance and identifying areas for improvement. By incorporating lessons learned from past experiences, consultants refine their approach, enhance their skills, and elevate the quality of their future engagements.

Building a Professional Network and Seeking Mentorship:

The power of connection and collaboration cannot be understated in the consulting world. Building a vibrant professional network opens doors to new opportunities, fosters knowledge sharing, and provides a platform for mentorship and support. Consultants actively engage in networking events, industry associations, and online communities to expand their reach and forge meaningful connections. They seek out mentors who can offer guidance, share wisdom, and provide valuable insights based on their own experiences. By leveraging the power of relationships, consultants tap into a wealth of knowledge and support that propels their growth and accelerates their success.

Embracing Lifelong Learning:

In the realm of continuous learning and professional development, one truth becomes evident: the journey is never-ending. Lifelong learning becomes a mindset, a way of approaching the world with curiosity and a hunger for knowledge. Effective consultants embrace a growth mindset, continuously seeking opportunities to learn and evolve. They invest in their own development through certifications, advanced degrees, and specialized training programs. They view each project as a chance to learn something new, to expand their horizons, and to challenge themselves. By embracing lifelong learning, consultants position themselves as perpetual students of their craft, always striving to reach new heights of excellence.

Continuous learning and professional development are not just buzzwords; they are the driving forces behind success in the consulting profession. By recognizing the importance of ongoing learning, staying updated with industry trends, seeking feedback, and building a vibrant professional network, consultants unlock the power to grow, transform, and make a lasting impact. As we conclude our journey through the world of consulting, we invite you to embrace the path of lifelong learning, to embrace change as an opportunity, and to fuel your growth with knowledge and passion. The possibilities are endless, and the journey awaits.

Case Study: Advancing Skills and Knowledge in the Digital Marketing Field

Case Study Background:

Sarah, a consultant specializing in digital marketing, understood the importance of continuous learning and professional development to stay ahead in the rapidly evolving digital landscape. Let's explore Sarah's journey and how she embraced continuous learning to enhance her skills and knowledge.

Case Study Scenario:

Sarah recognized that digital marketing practices and strategies constantly evolve. She realized the need to invest time and effort in continuous learning and professional development to remain competitive and provide valuable insights to her clients.

Step 1: Importance of Ongoing Learning and Skill Development:

Sarah recognized that ongoing learning and skill development were crucial to her success as a digital marketing consultant. She acknowledged that the field was dynamic and required staying updated with the latest trends, technologies, and best practices. Sarah understood that her ability to deliver effective strategies relied on her continuous growth and development.

Step 2: Staying Updated with Industry Trends and Best Practices:

To stay updated, Sarah regularly attended industry conferences, webinars, and workshops. She subscribed to reputable digital marketing publications, joined online communities and forums, and followed influential thought leaders in the field. By staying current with industry trends and best practices, Sarah could provide her clients with innovative and effective digital marketing strategies.

Step 3: Seeking Feedback and Incorporating Lessons Learned:

Sarah actively sought feedback from her clients, colleagues, and industry peers. She valued constructive criticism and used it as an opportunity for growth and improvement. Sarah also reflected on her past projects and campaigns, identifying lessons learned and areas for refinement. By incorporating feedback and lessons learned into her future endeavors, she continually enhanced her skills and expertise.

Step 4: Building a Professional Network and Seeking Mentorship:

Sarah recognized the value of building a professional network and seeking mentorship. She actively engaged with other digital marketing professionals through networking events, industry associations, and online communities. Sarah also sought guidance from experienced mentors who provided insights, advice, and guidance on her professional development journey. By leveraging the expertise and experiences of others, Sarah accelerated her growth and expanded her professional network.

Results and Impact:

Sarah's commitment to continuous learning and professional development had a significant impact on her career as a digital marketing consultant. By staying updated with industry trends and best practices, she consistently delivered innovative strategies to her clients. Seeking feedback and incorporating lessons learned allowed her to refine her approach and achieve better results. Building a professional network and seeking mentorship provided her with valuable connections and guidance throughout her career.

Sarah's dedication to continuous learning and professional development propelled her career forward. She became known as a go-to expert in the digital marketing field, attracting high-profile clients and gaining recognition for her expertise. Her ability to adapt to the evolving digital landscape and provide cutting-edge strategies ensured her long-term success as a consultant.

Key Takeaways:

- Continuous learning and skill development are vital for consultants to remain competitive in rapidly evolving industries.
- Staying updated with industry trends and best practices is essential to provide valuable insights and strategies to clients.
- Seeking feedback and incorporating lessons learned fosters professional growth and improvement.
- Building a professional network and seeking mentorship expands opportunities for learning and career advancement.

Conclusion:

Sarah's case study highlights the significance of continuous learning and professional development for consultants, particularly in dynamic fields such as digital marketing. By prioritizing ongoing learning, staying updated with industry trends, seeking feedback, and building a professional network, Sarah achieved remarkable success in her career. This case study underscores the importance of embracing a growth mindset and investing in professional development to deliver exceptional value to clients. In the following chapters, we will explore additional case studies that exemplify the power of continuous learning and professional growth in various consulting domains.

21

The Ethical Compass: Guiding Principles in Consulting

Chapter 20: The Ethical Compass: Guiding Principles in Consulting

Picture yourself standing at a crossroads, facing a myriad of choices that will shape your journey as a consultant. Which path will you take? The one paved with integrity, transparency, and trust, or the one fraught with ethical dilemmas and compromised values? In this chapter, we embark on an exciting exploration of the ethical considerations that underpin the consulting profession. Join us as we uncover the secrets to ethical excellence, learn how to navigate conflicts of interest, protect client confidentiality like a vault, and bravely tackle sensitive situations head-on.

Upholding Ethical Standards and Professional Conduct:

In the dynamic world of consulting, ethics serves as the compass that guides our every move. But what does it mean to uphold ethical standards and professional conduct? It means being a beacon of integrity, making decisions that align with our clients' best interests, and standing firm in the face of temptation. Through real-life examples and captivating stories, we'll unveil the importance of ethical conduct in building trust, credibility, and long-lasting relationships with our clients.

Dealing with Conflicts of Interest:

Ah, conflicts of interest—the treacherous waters where personal gain and professional duty collide. As consultants, we are not immune to their siren call. But fear not! We will equip you with the tools and strategies to navigate these murky waters like a seasoned sailor. We'll delve into captivating case studies, exposing the consequences of succumbing to conflicts of interest and showcasing the triumphs of consultants who chose the high road. Brace yourself for a thrilling adventure through the labyrinth of ethical decision-making.

Ensuring Client Confidentiality and Data Protection:

Imagine being entrusted with your client's deepest secrets, their proprietary information, and their most vulnerable aspirations. As guardians of confidentiality, it is our sacred duty to protect this treasure trove. Through gripping tales of intrigue and suspense, we'll reveal the methods and practices that keep client information locked away from prying eyes. Join us as we explore the world of data protection, cybersecurity, and the art of maintaining confidentiality in the age of digital espionage.

Navigating Sensitive and Challenging Situations:

In the world of consulting, we are often called upon to navigate treacherous terrains—situations fraught with sensitivity, conflicting interests, and cultural nuances. In this chapter, we embark on a thrilling expedition through these uncharted territories, armed with empathy, cultural intelligence, and a deep understanding of ethical considerations. We'll share heartwarming tales of consultants who turned seemingly impossible situations into triumphs, all while upholding their ethical compass. Get ready to unleash your inner adventurer and conquer the ethical challenges that lie ahead.

Continual Ethical Reflection and Improvement:

Ethics is not a stagnant concept etched in stone; it is a living, breathing force that requires constant nurturing and reflection. Join us in the pursuit of ethical excellence as we dive into the world of continual learning and improvement.

We'll introduce you to inspiring consultants who never rest on their laurels, constantly seeking feedback, mentorship, and opportunities for growth. Discover the power of self-reflection, industry collaboration, and staying ahead of the curve in an ever-changing ethical landscape.

As we conclude our exhilarating journey through the ethical considerations in consulting, let us not forget the profound impact our choices and actions have on our clients, our profession, and ourselves. The path to ethical excellence is not always easy, but the rewards are immeasurable. By upholding ethical standards, navigating conflicts of interest with grace, safeguarding client confidentiality like a vault, and fearlessly tackling sensitive situations, we become the ethical superheroes the consulting world needs. So, my fellow consultants, let us stand tall, guided by our ethical compass, and embark on a future where integrity reigns supreme.

22

Case Study: Upholding Integrity and Confidentiality in a High-Stakes Project

Case Study Background:

John, a seasoned consultant, found himself faced with a challenging project that required navigating ethical considerations with utmost care. Let's explore John's journey and how he successfully handled ethical dilemmas while upholding integrity and confidentiality.

Case Study Scenario:

John was hired by a large pharmaceutical company to assess their manufacturing processes and recommend improvements. The project involved sensitive information, proprietary formulas, and trade secrets. As the project progressed, John encountered several ethical considerations that required his careful attention and decision-making.

Step 1: Upholding Ethical Standards and Professional Conduct:

From the outset, John committed to upholding ethical standards and professional conduct. He understood the importance of integrity in his role as a consultant and the trust his clients placed in him. John diligently adhered to his professional code of ethics, which guided his decision-making throughout the project.

Step 2: Dealing with Conflicts of Interest:

During the project, John encountered a potential conflict of interest. He discovered that a close friend owned a competing pharmaceutical company. Recognizing the need for impartiality and transparency, John immediately disclosed the conflict to his client. He worked with the client to develop a plan to mitigate any potential bias and ensure that his recommendations were solely based on the best interests of the client.

Step 3: Ensuring Client Confidentiality and Data Protection:

Given the sensitive nature of the project, protecting client confidentiality and data became paramount. John implemented stringent security measures to safeguard the client's proprietary information. He obtained the necessary confidentiality agreements and ensured that all project team members were aware of their responsibilities regarding data protection. John also regularly communicated with the client about the measures in place to maintain confidentiality and sought their input on any additional precautions they desired.

Step 4: Navigating Sensitive and Challenging Situations:

As the project progressed, John encountered situations where he had to navigate sensitive matters. For instance, he discovered a potential safety issue in one of the manufacturing processes. Balancing the need for immediate action with the client's reputation, John tactfully and promptly communicated the issue to the appropriate stakeholders within the organization. He provided recommendations for rectifying the problem while maintaining the confidentiality of the information shared.

Results and Impact:

John's commitment to upholding ethical standards and addressing ethical considerations had a positive impact on the project and his client's trust. By navigating conflicts of interest transparently, ensuring client confidentiality, and addressing sensitive situations tactfully, John maintained his reputation as a trustworthy consultant.

The client appreciated John's integrity and professionalism throughout the project. They recognized his dedication to maintaining confidentiality, protecting their interests, and addressing ethical dilemmas promptly. John's ethical approach not only contributed to the success of the project but also strengthened the long-term relationship between him and the client.

Key Takeaways:

Upholding ethical standards and professional conduct is essential for consultants to maintain trust and integrity.

Addressing conflicts of interest transparently and pro-actively builds credibility with clients.

Protecting client confidentiality and data is crucial to maintain trust and safeguard sensitive information.

Navigating sensitive and challenging situations requires tact, open communication, and a commitment to ethical decision-making.

Conclusion:

John's case study emphasizes the significance of ethical considerations in consulting engagements. By upholding ethical standards, dealing with conflicts of interest transparently, ensuring client confidentiality, and navigating sensitive situations with integrity, John demonstrated his commitment to ethical conduct. This case study underscores the importance of ethics as a guiding principle for consultants and highlights the positive impact of ethical decision-making on client relationships and project outcomes.

In the following chapters, we will explore additional case studies that delve into the complexities of ethical considerations in different consulting contexts, further emphasizing the importance of ethical conduct and integrity in the consulting profession.

23

Conclusion: Embracing the Consultant's Odyssey

As we come to the end of our exhilarating expedition through the world of consulting, let us pause for a moment to reflect on the transformative journey we've undertaken together. Throughout this book, we've delved into the depths of knowledge and explored the intricate web of consulting principles, methodologies, and strategies. But beyond the theoretical realm, there lies a treasure trove of personal anecdotes, experiences, and lessons that shape us as consultants and inspire us to reach new heights.

Summarizing the Jewel's of Wisdom:

Gathered along the path we've traversed are the jewels of wisdom—those priceless insights that have the power to ignite our imagination, transform our thinking, and propel us towards excellence. As we summarize these gems, let us weave a tapestry of knowledge that transcends theory and resonates with the experiences we've shared.

But what good is knowledge without the vibrant hues of personal stories? It is through these anecdotes, rich with triumphs, challenges, and moments of revelation, that we infuse life into our learnings. Picture yourself immersed in captivating tales from the field, where consultants brave uncertainty, overcome obstacles, and leave indelible marks on the organizations they serve.

As we conclude this chapter, let us look towards the horizon and cast our gaze upon the horizon of future consultants, those budding visionaries who are preparing to embark on their own odyssey. It is our duty, as torchbearers of the consulting profession, to inspire and motivate these eager minds. Let us share our personal journeys, the transformative encounters that shaped our careers, and the pivotal moments that ignited our passion for organizational success.

But inspiration alone is not enough. We must instill in these future consultants a profound understanding of the lifelong commitment that lies ahead. Let us emphasize the importance of continuous learning, innovation, and adaptability in a world that evolves at lightning speed. Together, we can create a community of consultants who are not content with the status quo but relentlessly pursue excellence in every endeavor.

And so, dear fellow travelers, as we bid farewell to this book and each other, let us carry the torch of knowledge, experience, and inspiration with us on our individual paths. May we embrace the consultant's odyssey, armed with the wisdom we've acquired, the stories we've shared, and the unwavering belief that our collective efforts can shape a future where organizational success knows no bounds.

Safe travels, my companions, as you embark on your own extraordinary adventures as consultants. The journey awaits, and the world eagerly anticipates the impact you will make. Bon voyage!

24

Conclusion and Takeaway
by Dr Livingston

As we come to the end of this book, I want to express my gratitude for joining me on this enlightening journey into the realm of consulting. Throughout the chapters, we have explored the multifaceted aspects of this dynamic field, uncovering the strategies, skills, and insights that drive organizational success.

In concluding our exploration, I would like to emphasize a few key takeaways that I hope will resonate with you:

Consulting as a Catalyst for Growth: Consulting is not merely about offering advice or solutions; it is about being a catalyst for growth and transformation. Consultants have the privilege and responsibility of guiding organizations towards their full potential, fostering innovation, and driving positive change.

The Power of Relationships: Building strong relationships is at the heart of effective consulting. Trust, rapport, and effective communication lay the foundation for successful collaborations. As consultants, we must invest time and effort in understanding our clients' needs, engaging stakeholders, and facilitating consensus-building to achieve meaningful outcomes.

Embracing Change and Overcoming Resistance: Change is inevitable, and as consultants, we must embrace it and guide organizations through its complexities. Overcoming resistance requires empathy, effective communication, and a well-crafted implementation strategy. By instilling a culture of adaptability and continuous improvement, we can drive successful change initiatives.

Ethical Conduct and Professionalism: Upholding ethical standards is paramount in the consulting profession. We must navigate conflicts of interest, ensure client confidentiality and data protection, and make sound decisions rooted in integrity. By acting ethically and professionally, we build trust and credibility, forging lasting relationships with our clients.

Lifelong Learning and Growth: Consulting is a journey of continuous learning and growth. Staying updated with industry trends, seeking feedback, and embracing new skills and knowledge are essential for remaining at the forefront of the field. Building a professional network and seeking mentorship can further enhance our capabilities and broaden our perspectives.

As you reflect on the content of this book, I encourage you to apply these principles and insights in your own consulting endeavors. Let them serve as a compass as you navigate the ever-evolving landscape of organizational challenges and opportunities.

Remember, consulting is not just a profession—it is a calling. It requires dedication, passion, and a genuine desire to make a difference. With the right mindset, skills, and commitment, you have the power to shape organizations, empower individuals, and drive positive change in the world.

Thank you for joining me on this transformative journey. I wish you immense success and fulfillment as you embark on your own path as a consultant. May you inspire and empower those around you, leaving a lasting legacy of excellence and impact.

With heartfelt gratitude,
Dr. Livingston